Whisky &
Bourbon
COCKTAILS

David Biggs

Contents

INTRODUCTION

The spelling of the word 'Whisky' or 'Whiskey' is always worth a bar room debate. Officially there are only two kinds of drink that qualify for the spelling 'whisky', and those are Scotch whisky and Canadian Rye whisky. Reliable drinks dictionaries will confirm that all others are 'whiskey'. With the 'e'. Nobody seems able to offer a logical explanation for this. Apparently it's just the way it is and that's all there is to it. Although the best known whiskies come from Scotland, and the drink from that country is often referred to as 'Scotch', the Irish were making whiskey (with an 'e') for many years before the Scots ever discovered the noble art.

Before America imposed Prohibition in 1919, Irish Whiskey was by far the most popular spirit drink in the USA, with more than 400 brands available. Once alcohol was forbidden, however, illicit distillers tried to copy the good Irish stuff. They did so with rather nasty results and it took many years before whisky (or whiskey) regained its popularity after prohibition was lifted. By that time Scotch had firmly gained the upper hand in the market and has held it ever since. The American style of whiskey, first officially made in Kentucky and referred to as bourbon whiskey, must by law be made of at least 51 per cent of maize spirit and be matured in charred oak casks for at least four years, so it has certainly gained respectability and sophistication since those rough old Prohibition days.

Wherever it comes from and however it is spelled as a result, both whis-key and whisky are made by distilling fermented mash made from malted grain. It comes in a wide variety of styles, most of which are basically warm and smoky in character, so they are suited to making comforting winter drinks, rather than summer coolers, when used in cocktails.

Of course there are the exceptions, like the legendary mint julep, which is enjoyed as a delicious long drink that is almost pure whiskey on ice with a crush of fresh mint in it. Like all good cocktail recipes, the mint julep comes in several individual styles, according to the taste of its creator. Some like it with sugar and others add a splash of water. Some use the mint as a garnish while others prefer to crush it to infuse the drink with mint's fragrance.

There are two main ways of distilling whiskey. The traditional method is in a copper pot-still, as used in the production of the legendary Single Malt whiskies that have become connoisseur's drinks and cost an arm and a leg. The cheaper method is to use a continuous column still that produces a more neutral spirit, and is then usually blended with the pot-still stuff to make most of the proprietary brands. The good news here is that there are plenty of reasonably inexpensive blended whiskies available for use in cocktails, so you don't need to cause your Scottish ancestors to turn in their graves because you add lemonade and a cherry to your 16-year-old Lagavulin.

In most whisky-based cocktail recipes, the whisky – or whiskey – part can be either Scotch or bourbon. Usually one or the other is specified and this merely gives an indication of the origin of the recipe. Purists will probably hold up their hands in horror at this sacrilege, but in all seriousness it would take a very rare palate to distinguish between the two once the bartender has added the club soda, gomme syrup, angostura bitters, slices of lemon and cherry on a stick.

As with all cocktail recipes, the whole idea is to relax and enjoy, without any fuss or pretence. Feel free to vary the proportions and ingredients as you like. Insist on having Kentucky bourbon, Irish whiskey or Highland malt if that's what pleases you. It's your palate and you're entitled to keep it happy any way you wish.

Highball tumbler

Cocktail glass

Lowball tumbler

Wine goblet

Classic
Collection

Scotch Old Fashioned

Here's a cocktail that adds a bittersweet touch to whisky. No doubt the Scots would disapprove strongly of any addition to what they believe is already the perfect drink, but if you're not Scottish you might like to try it.

A cube of sugar
A few dashes of Angostura bitters
Two measures of Scotch whisky
Ice cubes

- *Soak a sugar cube in Angostura bitters and place it in the bottom of a lowball glass.*
- *Add just enough water to dissolve the sugar and then pour in the measures of whisky. Stir gently and drop in two ice cubes.*

Three Rivers

Invented in Canada and often known by its French name, Trois Rivieres, this drink has become an international classic.

Ice cubes

Two parts whiskey
(preferably Canadian)

One part Dubonnet

One part Triple Sec

- *Place four or five ice cubes in a cocktail shaker and add the whiskey, Dubonnet and Triple Sec.*
- *Shake well and strain into a lowball glass.*
- *Serve ungarnished.*

Rob Roy

This drink named after the famous Scottish hero should be poured whenever a toast is drunk to heroes.

Ice cubes
Two dashes of Angostura bitters
One generous part Scotch whisky
One equally generous part
sweet vermouth
A twist of orange

- *Place two ice cubes in a lowball glass and splash in two dashes of bitters.*
- *Add the whisky and vermouth, garnish with a twist of orange and serve.*

Waldorf

By using different blends of whisky you can create a whole range of different Waldorf cocktails. Traditionally, bourbon is used.

Crushed ice
Two parts bourbon
One part Pernod
One part sweet vermouth
A dash of Angostura bitters

- *Place a scoop of crushed ice in a bar glass and add the bourbon, Pernod, sweet vermouth and Angostura bitters.*
- *Stir well, strain into a chilled cocktail glass.*

Irish Coffee

This is a fine alternative to ordinary coffee at the end of a good meal. The Irish have long been putting a dash of whiskey in their tea and calling it Irish tea, but the barman changed the recipe slightly to appeal to the American airmen who were using Shannon Airport as their base during World War II. Americans have always preferred coffee to tea. You can actually buy an Irish liqueur called Irish Velvet, which is based on Irish whiskey, black coffee and sugar. It's not as pleasant, or as much fun, as making your own.

One part Irish whiskey
Five parts strong, black coffee
A teaspoon of brown sugar
One part thick cream

- *Pour the Irish whiskey and hot coffee into a warmed Irish coffee glass, which is sometimes a goblet with a handle like a teacup and sometimes shaped like a large wineglass.*
- *Add brown sugar to taste and stir gently until it is dissolved.*
- *Trickle the cream over the back of a teaspoon onto the surface of the coffee.*

Manhattan

Like so many of life's great pleasures, the classical Manhattan cocktail is simple. It also has interesting variations. Here's the easiest version.

Three parts blended whiskey
One part sweet vermouth
A maraschino cherry
Crushed ice

- *Fill a mixing glass with crushed ice.*
- *Add the whiskey and vermouth to the mixing glass and stir well.*
- *Strain into a cocktail glass and garnish with the cherry.*
- *To make a Dry Manhatten, substitute dry vermouth for the sweet vermouth.*

Night Owl

This is a drink for the early hours of morning, when the city's still and the music's mellow.

Four parts of bourbon
One part of lemon juice
One part of triple sec
A dash of angostura bitters
Chilled soda water
Cracked ice

- *Swirl the bitters about in a highball glass to coat the sides and then fill it with cracked ice.*
- *Add the whiskey, lemon juice and triple sec and stir gently.*
- *Top up with soda water and stir again, still gently.*
- *Sip while watching the sun rise.*

Tipperary

Here's the perfect cocktail to serve on St Patrick's Day when you've had your fill of green beer.

One part Irish whiskey
One part sweet vermouth
Half a part of green chartreuse
Ice cubes

- *Place all the ingredients in a cocktail shaker with a few cubes of ice.*
- *Shake well, strain into a cocktail glass, then serve and enjoy!*

Whisky Mac

This is a very simple drink to mix, but has become something of a classic.

One part Scotch whisky
One part ginger wine
Crushed ice

- *Add the two ingredients to a measure of crushed ice in a cocktail shaker.*
- *Shake well and then strain into a chilled cocktail glass.*

Scotch Mist

The simplest version of Scotch Mist is simply Scotch on the rocks with a twist of lemon zest over it. This hot version is served in a tea cup and is known, for some strange reason, as the 'English' Scotch mist. It's probably something to do with the tea.

One part Scotch whisky
Three parts freshly brewed
Ceylon tea
Honey
Thick cream

- *Mix the whisky and tea together and add the honey to taste, stirring over a low heat until almost (but not quite) boiling.*
- *Pour into small (demitasse) coffee cups and float a teaspoon of cream onto the surface of each drink.*

Treasures
From The
Deep South

Mint Julep

A good Mint Julep is a drink for the wealthy. Not many people today will be able to afford the 'tankard of bourbon' that forms the basis of the drink. But for those occasions when you do feel like a millionaire, here's the recipe.

Crushed ice
A tankard of bourbon
A teaspoon of caster sugar
Two tablespoons of water
A teaspoon of Barbados rum
A large bunch of freshly picked mint

- *Place a cup of crushed ice in a pitcher and add the bourbon, caster sugar, water and rum. Stir well.*
- *Crush the mint leaves lightly to release the flavour and place them in a serving jug.*
- *Strain the contents of the bar glass into the jug, add four or five ice cubes and serve in lowball glasses.*

New Orleans

Many cocktails got their names from the places where they were invented. This one obviously originated in the southern United States and evokes images of the Mardi Gras and Dixieland jazz.

Crushed ice
Three parts bourbon
One part Pernod
Three dashes of Angostura bitters
A dash of anisette
A teaspoon of sugar syrup (or less to taste)
Ice cubes
A twist of lemon

- *Place a scoop of crushed ice in a cocktail shaker and add the bourbon, Pernod, bitters, anisette and sugar syrup.*
- *Shake vigorously and strain into a lowball glass filled with ice cubes.*
- *Garnish with a twist of lemon before serving.*

Comfortable Screw

Southern Comfort is a truly delicious orange-and-peach-flavoured whiskey that is produced in the southern United States.

Ice cubes
One part Southern Comfort
Six parts fresh orange juice
A banana

- *Place six ice cubes in a cocktail shaker and add the Southern Comfort and orange juice.*
- *Shake well and strain into a lowball glass.*
- *Garnish with the banana and serve.*

Key Biscayne

Here's an attractive little cocktail with a purely American origin.

> Three parts bourbon whiskey
> One part Curaçao
> One part sweet vermouth
> Juice of half a lime
> A sprig of mint

- *Add all ingredients, except the mint, to crushed ice in a cocktail shaker.*
- *Shake well and strain into a chilled cocktail glass.*
- *Decorate with a sprig of mint.*

Nob Hill

You can play with the balance between sweet and sour here to adjust the taste and reach your perfect palate cleanser.

Two parts rye whiskey
One part grapefruit juice
Honey to taste
Ice cubes

- *Place all the ingredients in a cocktail shaker with a handful of ice cubes.*
- *Shake very well and then strain into a cocktail glass.*
- *Serve ungarnished.*

Martha Washington

We don't know whether Martha actually drank this, but it certainly keeps her name alive.

Two parts rye or bourbon
One part cherry liqueur
A splash of lemon juice
Sugar syrup to taste
One maraschino cherry
Crushed ice

- *Mix all the liquid ingredients with crushed ice in a blender or cocktail shaker and strain into a cocktail glass.*
- *Garnish with the cherry.*

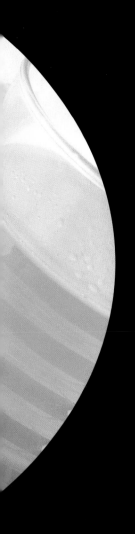

Sting In
The Tail

Leprechaun

It is said that if you capture a leprechaun he will grant you a wish, and who could wish for more than this merry drink?

Ice cubes
One part Irish whiskey
    (a large one, of course)
Two parts tonic water
Lemon peel

- *Place two ice cubes in a highball glass and add the whiskey and tonic.*
- *Stir reverently and twist the lemon peel over it. Drop in the twisted peel and serve.*

Sazerac

This romantic drink derived its name from the company importing brandy from France, Sazerac du Forge et Fils. Later, rye whiskey replaced the brandy in the recipe, but the name remained the same.

A lump of sugar
A dash of Angostura bitters
Ice cubes
Two generous parts rye whiskey
A dash of Pernod
A twist of lemon

- *Soak the sugar lump in Angostura bitters and place it in a cooled lowball glass with an ice cube.*
- *Add the whiskey and stir well.*
- *Add the Pernod and twist the lemon rind over the glass.*

Everything But

Now here's a truly dangerous drink. Apart from the alcohol, it also has other exciting ingredients, such as caster sugar, citrus and a whole egg, that only go into the most daring drinks. No wonder it's called Everything But – the missing words are probably 'the Kitchen Sink'. It's actually more of a joke drink than a serious one. When you ask a guest what he wants and he says, 'Everything', this is it. Here goes.

Ice cubes
One part rye whiskey
One part dry gin
One part lemon juice
One part orange juice
One egg
Half a part apricot brandy
One teaspoon caster sugar

- *Place six ice cubes in a cocktail shaker and add the whiskey, gin, lemon and orange juice, egg, apricot brandy and sugar to taste.*
- *Shake until smooth and velvety and strain into a highball glass.*

- *Add ice cubes if required.*
- *If you really want to go the whole hog, frost the rim of the glass with caster sugar before pouring the drink.*

The Boilermaker

It could be argued that this rough-and-ready drink is not a cocktail, as it is taken in two parts. It certainly is a mixed drink, though. I've seen it drunk in several countries, by drinkers in various stages of alcoholic merriment.

A shot glass of blended whisky
A mug of lager beer

- *The shot glass of whisky is usually swallowed in a single gulp, followed by a glass of beer. Sometimes the whisky and beer are mixed in a glass or tankard and drunk together.*

Rattlesnake

One of the many slang names for illicit moonshine liquor was 'snake juice', which probably referred to the rough mountain-distilled spirit. This is a refined version, using bourbon.

> **Crushed ice**
> **Two parts bourbon**
> **One teaspoon of lemon juice**
> **One teaspoon of sugar syrup**
> **Half an egg white**
> **Several dashes of Pernod**

- *Place a scoop of crushed ice in a cocktail shaker and add the bourbon, lemon juice, sugar syrup, egg white and Pernod.*
- *Shake vigorously for 10 seconds or more and strain it into a chilled lowball glass.*

Whippet

Here's a tangy little drink to add some spice to a perfect evening.

Three parts blended Scotch whisky
One part peppermint schnapps
One part crème de cacao
Plenty of ice

- *Place a few cubes of ice in a cocktail shaker and add the three ingredients.*
- *Shake well and strain over a lowball glass filled with ice cubes.*

Hot Brick Toddy

Some would describe this drink more as medication than a cocktail. It's said to be a wonderful cure for colds. On the other hand, why wait until you're sick?

Three dollops of rye whiskey
A teaspoon of unsalted butter
A teaspoon of brown sugar
A pinch of cinnamon
Boiling water

- *First, dissolve the butter and brown sugar in a little boiling water.*
- *Then add the whiskey and cinnamon.*
- *Stir well and add the rest of the water, still stirring, until you reach the desired strength.*
- *No prescription is needed.*

Refreshing
Coolers

Lady Hunt

An elegant and delicious cocktail that is tangy and crisp in character, but also gently mellow.

Three parts malt whisky
One part Tia Maria
One part Amaretto
Juice of half a lemon
A dash of egg white
Ice cubes
A slice of orange
A maraschino cherry

- *Place all the ingredients with the exception of the orange slice and cherry into a cocktail shaker with four ice cubes and shake briskly.*
- *Strain into a cocktail glass and decorate with the slice of orange and the maraschino cherry.*

Spirit of Scotland

This cocktail is most appropriately named as Drambuie is made of whisky, heather and honey. What could be more Scottish?

Crushed ice
Two parts Scotch whisky
One part Drambuie
Half a part lemon juice

- *Place a scoop of crushed ice in a blender or cocktail shaker and add the whisky, Drambuie and lemon juice.*
- *Blend everything together briskly and strain into a cocktail glass.*

Clubman Cocktail

Irish Mist is a liqueur based on Irish whiskey flavoured with herbs and honey and produced in Tulach Mhor, Ireland. The Clubman is a very colourful drink, guaranteed to start the conversation flowing.

Ice cubes
One part Irish Mist
Four parts orange juice
A dessertspoon of egg white
A dash of blue Curaçao

- *Place four ice cubes in a cocktail shaker and add the Irish Mist, orange juice and egg white.*
- *Shake briskly and strain into a lowball glass.*
- *Carefully trickle the blue Curaçao down the sides of the glass (you might like to use a straw) to create a marbled effect.*

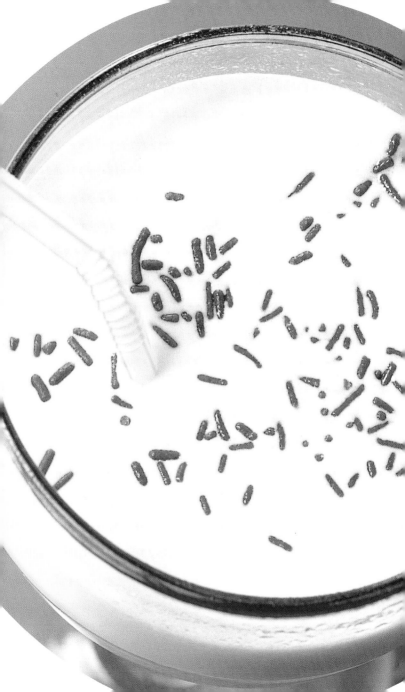

Dom Pedro

This delicious little cocktail has become a firm favourite on many restaurant menus. The strange thing about it is that nobody seems to know who Dom Pedro was, or how this sweet delight got its name. There are two basic versions, one using whisky and the other using Kahlua. Both are delicious.

Vanilla ice cream
A generous measure of whisky or Kahlua
Chocolate vermicelli

- *Fill a lowball glass or goblet with soft vanilla ice cream and pour the whisky or Kahlua over it.*
- *Whip briskly with a fork until well blended and serve garnished with a sprinkling of chocolate vermicelli. It is usual to provide a long bar spoon to help reach the bottom bits.*

White Heather

Bartenders from all around the world compete regularly at international gatherings where new drinks are tried, discussed and judged. This award-winning recipe, invented by barman Rodney Brock, specified the brand of each of the ingredients, but we leave it to readers to select their own. It really is a wonderful drink.

Ice cubes
One part Scotch whisky
One part crème de banane
One part crème de cacao
Two parts thin cream
Nutmeg

- *Place three ice cubes in a cocktail shaker and add all the ingredients except the nutmeg.*
- *Shake well and strain into a cocktail glass.*
- *Grate nutmeg over the drink and serve.*

Whisky Fix

This is a cocktail that's said to clear the head and act as a very good pick-me-up after a long and hard day.

Two parts blended Scotch whisky
One part fresh lemon juice
Crushed ice
Castor sugar
Pieces of fresh fruit, depending on the season

- *Fill a collins glass with crushed ice and add the lemon juice, Scotch and castor sugar.*
- *Stir well and then serve, garnished with a few cubes of fresh fruit.*

Whiskey Frost

This is an interesting drink that needs a little preparation time. Before the party, freeze an ice tray containing pure lemon juice. When this has frozen, take:

One part bourbon
One part medium cream sherry
One part port
A dash of sugar syrup
A slice of lemon

- *In a cocktail shaker, mix the liquid ingredients with a few ice cubes and strain into a lowball glass.*
- *Add two of the lemon ice cubes and garnish with a slice of lemon on the rim of the glass.*

Skibbereen Tonic

A fresh little Irish drink this, and mighty easy to prepare as well.

A helping of good Irish whiskey
Indian quinine tonic water
Lemon peel
Cubes of ice

- *Place a few cubes of ice in a lowball glass and pour in the whiskey and tonic water.*
- *Stir gently and twist the lemon peel over the drink to release the oils.*
- *Drop the peel in and serve.*

Normandy Jack

Obviously this drink gets its name from the calvados or apple brandy, which is a speciality of Normandy.

Two parts blended Scotch whisky
One part calvados or apple brandy
Half a part of lemon juice
Sugar syrup to taste
Crushed ice

- *Place some crushed ice in a cocktail shaker and add all the ingredients.*
- *Shake well and strain into a chilled cocktail glass.*
- *Serve without garnish.*

First published in 2004
by New Holland Publishers
London • Cape Town
Sydney • Auckland
www.newhollandpublishers.com

86 Edgware Road, London,
W2 2EA, United Kingdom

80 McKenzie Street,
Cape Town, 8001, South Africa

14 Aquatic Drive, Frenchs Forest,
NSW 2086, Australia

218 Lake Road, Northcote,
Auckland, New Zealand

Publishing Managers
Claudia dos Santos & Simon Pooley
Commissioning Editor Alfred LeMaitre
Concept Design Geraldine Cupido
Designer Jeannette Streicher
Editor Nicky Steenkamp
Stylist Justine Kiggen
Production Myrna Collins

Reproduction by
Resolution Colour Pty Ltd, Cape Town

Printed and bound in
Singapore by Tien Wah Press (Pte) Ltd

ISBN 1 84330 716 2

2 4 6 8 10 9 7 5 3 1